Stone To Heart

The Grey Zone

Syed Taha Hussain

BookLeaf
Publishing

India | USA | UK

Made with ❤ on the BookLeaf Publishing Platform

www.bookleafpub.in

www.bookleafpub.com

Dedication

To the people and moments that touch lives.

Preface

"Stone To Heart : The Grey Zone" is a collection of poems about shared memories and experience with people having an impact in life. The ups and downs in life help to grow as an individual. Sailing through these lines, you may find a renewed appreciation for the simple relatable moments.

Acknowledgements

Heartfelt gratitude to the world for being an endless source of inspiration to write. Special thanks to the readers for their love for poetry. Your support and appreciation are deeply valued.

1. Feels alright

Made my existence feel trivial
Helped their ashes rise
Sometimes got them buried alive

Years passed by
One day the sun rose bright
Stayed in the shade
But it felt alright

Told myself, they even advised
Now is the time to step into light and take a bite
Dark and bitter, I asked why
Voices forcing to act again and be grateful as I am

Don't mind sunsets
But they need to be mine
Else I stay in the shade
Because it feels alright!

2. Tribe

Say please take care, just to sound nice
Bring wrath, if it will never cross back your mind
Play it on loop and you get their kind
Craving for something you aren't sure you like
Find another supper because I need to unburn mine

Ceaseless thunderbolts and flooding streets
Astonished like you made a secret dream
No war, kept calm, held tight
And you say I advertised

A silent clap to get peace close
Made a scene like the tropics froze
Goodwill ain't common, know it for a fact
Can make you feel sorry to not match their vibe
Remember, you are just not their tribe!

3. Perfect profile

Promises were made
Some stood most failed
Took me a million smiles
Made a perfect profile

Kept in touch, same talk, no rush
Felt more and more pushed
Like fire catching the bush
Was it you or my pride
To keep you happy or drive me mad

Meant to complete the puzzle
Never got the right fit
My intentions or their preferences
Which one was a lie ?

Had I screamed too loud
Would the board break or make a match
Your reasons since the start
Makes me rethink our path
It was you, not my pride
To keep you happy and not drive me mad

4. Only option

People criticize like its their only art
For something that shouldn't concern a lot
Tried blocking way and made a plot
Like I took away their only shot

Got all the unasked sage advice
Wished they choke on it and die
Can't call it a decision or a choice
When its the only option to abide

Stayed on the shore, not to overload
A leech to the only one I adore
Holding oceans like pressure on coal
Removed an ounce, hoping to save a soul

Stayed away, let the party end
Don't need a crowd for me to blend
What just felt a little sneak peek
Had paved a way for the ocean to leak

Taken aback for I didn't stutter
Necessity for one could be a luxury for another
Can't call it a decision or a choice
When its the only option to abide

5. No time to cry

Knowing you was empowering
Went bonkers for a glimpse

Changed the system like a king
Still no potion for your sting

Found no solace in wisdom
Is loving you a dictum

If caterpillars can butterfly
There's just no time to cry

6. Endgame

Pulled me up just to get stacked in trash
Left me there like it was a giftwrap
Far from home, got a broken bone
Heard I had it all coming along

Relentless drama, no trust, no charm
Caused her an unintended harm
Tearing our worlds with no band-aid around
Hoping
Realizing what's wrong, should be the endgame for all

Stayed indoors till I felt more broke
Can forget one pain only when a better one rose
Asked everyone, knocked door to door
Stop being paranoid, leave the cosmos alone

Checked every heartbeat before taking a step
Brought more disruption with every flutter I felt
Made me indifferent to almost all
Hoping
Realizing what's wrong, should be the end game for all

7. Dark sun

To shine you needn't be a star
Happy needn't always be the end

Broken doesn't mean not working
Perfect doesn't mean you like

Help may not be the solution
Its absence could make you a knight

With sunshines we are all possessed
Until the sun rises from the west!

8. Blind to love

Completed a task, got the paycheck
Stepping stone felt like a mountain trek
Long due vacation to keep me sound
Didn't stop you from buzzing around

Got back soon and worked nonstop
Draining my blood to its very last drop
Why are the people we love so blind ?
Are they naive or just unkind

Got overwhelmed and fell when close
Laying down like a breathing corpse
Pictured you dancing on my grave
Did you not notice, or was I brave

Couldn't take the leap you expected
Lost my time, but no one regretted
Why are the people we love so blind ?
Are they naive or just unkind

9. Darkside

9

Radiant colours and dazzling smile
Me in my sorrows, never ending lies

Karma came by
Let you go, saw your good side
Held me tight, like I had forsaken mine

You laughed at me till you cried
Forgot, its for all, mine just came to apprise

One day, the sun will rise
By my side
We shall shine so bright
You will stare in fright
And see your dark side

10. Blame game

At the seacoast, claiming the whole world
Sand castles got washed away, leaving behind my ghost
Prospects immersed under circumstances
Gazes turned into glances

Broken souls can make you whole
Picture perfects love their payroll
Why do I blame you for all I got ?
Despite all the love you gave, but never got

All mine in black and white
Still feels like a stolen prize
Helped me climb when I liked laying low
Left to find cover
Couldn't we all just navigate though ?

Asked me to dream, not fantasize
Hope, not expect
Now can I blame you for all I got ?
As I needed compassion, not love

11. Stars aligned

Made breakfast, pickle and cake
Went miles away to keep me safe
Like I wore a superhero cape
When will my stars align oh lord!
Shift me to there or just use your sword

Could skip a meal or two
Stay a bit longer, lets be true
You need me and I need you
Together we can make the stars queue
On every planet of all the galaxies I knew

12. Selfless love

Strong enough to breakdown walls that reach the sky
With a warmth, not a billion bonfires could buy
Wanting us to dream as high as we could
Shelved yours, feeling that you should

A shield guarding from all the striking arrows
Not of iron nor of stone, but made of love, a selfless one
If one missed and gave a nick so small
The shield always got ten times strong
Blessed to witness your selfless love
My inspiration, my strength, my world

Always asked more like it was my birthright
Now making few bucks feels like a dark night
Curious to find the dreams you wrote
Found it, with only one enclosed

Crossing it would be a cakewalk I thought
But all it read was for us to outshine the stars
Not the diamonds we gifted that could shatter
Its only the thought that matters
Blessed to witness your selfless love
My inspiration, my strength, my world

13. Crownless king

Picked up the crown you left for charity
Built an empire far from your reach
Labelled it luck and you cursed me
If it were you, wouldn't you call it destiny
Is your charity now your only longing ?

Usurped my throne, like you defeated me
I stepped down, thinking you could heal
A gesture for which, got named a crownless king
Your curse for sure had a play in it
If it were you, wouldn't you call it destiny
Is your charity now your only longing ?

14. Depression aesthetic

14

Bonding more isn't as easy you mock
Took the long path, made small talk

When pride's on hold, cringe feels cool
All in vain, now more insane

Labelling me a monster, was quite sympathetic
For just
Withdrawal from my depression aesthetic

Fit me in, I don't mould, I just break
Not very unique, just to stay in the game

Comfort zones being friendly fire enabled
Makes me irrelevant, insignificant, unstable

Labelling me a monster, was quite sympathetic
For just
Withdrawal from my depression aesthetic

15. Blossom

In the morning, when the trees start to blossom

Like a kid waiting for his mom's return
Like summer craving to burst the cloud
Like the blind hoping to see the world

Don't ask me to enjoy the moment for once
My moments depend on the moments to come

Like a deer waiting to make a hunt
Like waves wishing to cross the shore
Like a whale hoping to walk the earth

Don't ask me to enjoy the moment for once
My moments depend on the moments to come

In the morning, when the trees start to blossom

16. Delusions of heart

16

A story you tell to keep them quiet
They listen close and add their checkpoint
Why face detention when there's no crime
All I needed to know was that eagles can fly

You add a few lines
Just to make the end sound nice
Out of love or to console your mind
All I ever knew was to reach sky high

Delusions of heart are hard to leave
Even when the mind is ready to accept reality

17. Saccharine soul

Made an identity, not everyone can endorse
Had it all like you hit a jackpot
Deep down craving to cut all bonds
Can't say why, but it felt all mutual
Your saccharine soul couldn't hurt a fly
Made me fall more for you that night

Waiting for you on the railway track
Missing the bond we never had
Called you saying its just for a hi!
Saw you on your journey and it felt like a final bye!

Do not think you aren't worth my time
Having you was like a lifeline
I just don't feel like being me anymore
Wish I could do more

18. Settings default

Been too nice, said its alright
Couldn't stop, I swear I tried
A comparison with sharp claws
Only when it fits your cause
If not, I don't exist at all

I can't scream, I can't revolt
Welcome to my settings default

Received one for a thousand
And you brag out loud
A limit is something
You conveniently forgot
You ask, "Where is the trust we knew ?"
Would it exist if I were you ?

I can't scream, I can't revolt
Welcome to my settings default

19. Its gotta be me

Engrossed in our daily routine
You took a U-turn, left me on seen
Blessings I couldn't guarantee
Hold me tight and set me free
Only if I could see
You ain't the solution, its gotta be me

I lashed out, you betrayed me
Whining like a child
A ghost gone wild
Mutual sorry has no end
Unless the goal is to not be friends
Only if I could see
You ain't the solution, its gotta be me
Its gotta be me

20. Road sign

Entrapped in the web
I helped you create
You fumble, you are dead
If life were a game with luck behind bars
You would know
When you ascend or when you fall

In my own bubble
Can't see your pity smile
Barged in, reminding me of me
Like I am not mine
Kept focus and beat
For an end I couldn't design

Is there a road sign ?
To outline a timeline
To afford a sunshine

21. Heart to stone

Asked to overcome my low self esteem
Trying to, filled me up with gasoline

Just a little friction could burn me down
Did moon walk on cotton balls

Unadventurous, secure and sound
Ah! What a life, I can sham it all

Heart turning stone gave the spark I dread
Made me shine for a moment, before I finally fell

www.ingramcontent.com/pod-product-compliance
Lightning Source LLC
Chambersburg PA
CBHW071315130726
47997CB00007B/2560